Flows Through You

Where small feelings run deep

Stuti Srivastava

BookLeaf Publishing

India | USA | UK

Made with ❤ on the BookLeaf Publishing Platform
www.bookleafpub.in
www.bookleafpub.com

Dedication

To the landscape within—
where emotions run like rivers
and growth rises like trees—
your touch shaped each word
that found its way here.

Preface

To feel deeply is often seen as too much.
But in these pages, it is *just enough.*
This collection was born from moments that look so
small yet feels so deep.
The smile of getting that first coffee sip just right to
The laughter that hides behind *"Hello!! Papa"*,
the quiet ache in *"The Invisible Cage"*,
or the longing wrapped in a single line of *"Soul-Ties"*.
Each poem is a small truth I didn't know how else to say.
Being sensitive—*extremely* so—is not a flaw.
It is the lens through which I see, breathe, and break
beautifully.
This book is a way of nurturing that gift.
Of saying, *yes, I feel too much—and I'm learning to love
that about myself.*
Some pieces will speak to you.
Others may simply sit beside you in silence.
Both are enough.
Welcome to the soft corners of emotion.
Let's Connect the dots—
But gently.

Acknowledgements

I am deeply grateful to my parents and my family—for being my foundation, my greatest strength, and the quiet belief behind every step I've taken. Your love, trust, and values continue to guide me in ways I can never fully put into words. You are the home I carry with me.

To my closest friends—thank you for the laughter that held me together, for the late-night pep talks, the spontaneous wisdom, and for cheering me on like I was already there. You've made the journey lighter, louder, and full of joy.

To the quiet signs from the universe—thank you for showing up just when I needed a nudge, a pause, or a little magic.

And to myself—for beginning, again and again. For feeling everything, and still choosing to stay open.

And finally, to you, dear reader—thank you for being here. I hope these pages feel like a warm cup of something familiar, a soft place to land, or simply a quiet companion on a day you needed one.

With love
Stuti Srivastava

1.. Connect the dots

So cliché to hear this
Yet impossible to dismiss

Do I have to linger in the past and connect
For unseen vision of future to resurrect

Or maybe to connect all lost dots within me
To find and embrace the real me

As I started to connect the dots
The crust and trough reminding life is in morse code

So difficult to understand yet so easy to live
It's like a gift from god, which makes sense at the very
end

Maybe it is very logical to make maps
And emotional to live with clamps

I am just a wanderer

In this mystic life of a gatherer

2. They might Bite you!

How does it feel to be chosen?
I bet you thinking of god's token

But by an animal
A feeling so whimsical

They rub themselves next to you
As they welcome a new member to their crew

The look of pure love with no conditions
Like loving you is their only soulful mission

She confides within my arms
Safe from all wordly harms

Nothing goes in my brain
No stress in my chest, just joy in my lane

Feels like a moral responsibility to set them free
Break the chains and let them be

It's their world, as much as it is ours
Sharing the skies, trees and stars

Greet them as they come
Without chaining them and making them succumb

3. Madhusudhan , you there?

He met me when my shadows were cold and dry,
And all I was longing for a shoulder to cry.

Shadows were darker than color black,
The chains holding me were making me lose my track.

I was under a veil and soul in a shrodinger's box,
He came in with a bright light, calling everything a hoax.

Softened my rock hard heart and took me to calmer
waters,
With his mature smile ,made the surroundings warmer....

Not ready , but took a leap of faith one last time..
I went to a journey within me ,with him as a fantastic
guide.

Killing all my fears, insecurities,
And embracing my maturity in immaturity

He made me fall in love with me ,
Seeing him happy was the only intention left in me.

His eyes has a deep ocean of patience,
Which holds me strong in his absence.

He is my mirror
My mirror staring back at me.....

Although there's so much distance
But we have a magic in trust with natural acceptance

And just his presence,
Makes me remember my motivation with a sweet
essence.

4. Umm coffee??

The first sip of the day
Differentiates black and white from grey

How do I explain this?
The feeling that fills

It's like seeing reflection in dew
and mesmerizing as color blue

A talk over coffee?
No sorry, not sorry

Rather not talk than miss this experience
Rather be clear than mysterious

An experience so elite
Syncing with heartbeat on repeat

"Yeah the coffee tastes good"
The answer often misunderstood

5. I don't want to do this anymore!!

Ever felt so frustrated
Urges to run away are created

Just to leave everything behind
To some shady place to hide

When confrontation is too heavy
Not knowing when to be ready

But what if I don't run away?
Face it with courage and stay

Will these urges still haunt me?
Or will I be finally free

What if it's me that scares
The morals crashing which I really care

But how will I improve?
Unless this time I stop the move

6. Mummy, you know what happened today???

Still missing sitting on kitchen counter
As I see you making rotis rounder and rounder

The strength of character comes from you
When you teach me how to be true

Geography is our favourite subject
where we effortlessly and amazingly connect

You are like my sink
and your lap a paradise where I just don't think

Every touch so heavenly
Filling my entire existence with serenity

So beautiful in a saree
Unlike a menace like me, on contrary

I love you with all my heart
Which is way beyond charts

7. Hello!! Papa

Held my arms around him
While going on a trip

From teaching math on dining table
To teaching me how to slit a cable

We all grew up together
It's a bond of forever

Bringing my favourite biscuit
Even when mummy puts a limit

I take your teachings as I go
Helping me everytime I get low

No one says this enough
But dad you are rough and tough

Helping me through every chaos
Without experiencing any loss

8. Are you mountain or beach person?

Does the ocean wave at you?
As it fills your lungs with salt

A feeling so pure and serene
None other than being on a beach

The gurgles of water
Intensifying as dusk gets closer

Huge enough to hug the sun at dusk and dawn
Spreading the warmth even when the sun is gone

Talk about true love
One like sun and ocean

So far apart
Yet beautiful when seen together at horizon

Connecting us all together
To ocean from a small river

9. Love is Divine

I remember how I felt when I heard your name
I turned back for a glimpse overcoming all shame

You stayed with me for long dark nights
Giving hope that next day, it will be very bright

I know how hard it was for you at times
But we had it all figured out like a fine wine

You are in one of my deepest corners of soul
Like a controller to a gaming console

I would cherish you when you won't love yourself
So that you can see from the eyes of the beholder herself

10. Drops on a Beach

I was standing with my bare feet
Waiting for our eyes to meet

On a lonely beach, but you never turned
and all these feelings in my stomach churned

I swear I would do anything to stop you
But I can't let myself turn blue

You say we are done as we watched the waves
But I still remember cold coffee was one of your faves

How did we become this, I had no clue
As I saw dead love on sand and how the vultures flew

I was stranded with teardrops making wet holes in sand
Soon I see more raindrops on my hand

Guessing someone up there is lonely too

I picked up all my pieces and transformed to something
new

11. Kindness for Self

Hating myself enough for past
Making it difficult to remember when I smiled last

Is this hate necessary?
When love is in the air

Trying to change everything
And forgetting how to bloom in spring

Is it really hate or just sadness
That I lacked self awareness

Of not choosing myself first
While life moves between trough and crust

Sitting with oneself is tormenting
But it's better than lamenting

Embracing to learn one's mistakes
Building a foundation no one can break

It was very hard at first
Easier when I started to forgive and trust

12. Knock Knock who is there?

This time when sadness
Knocks on my door in my mess

I didn't take a broom
To kick him out of my room

This time, I invited him and
Offered him food that was so bland

He smiled and asked
"Why do you detest me like I am plague?"

I answered angrily
"Cause you make me cry intensely"

He simply opened a huge scroll
Some gibberish, some symbols which obviously made
my eyes roll

Irritated I asked "What do you want now?"
Caressing my hair, he said just learn these symbols for
now

Those symbols came as form of learnings
As an experience's earning

First time I sat and thought
All this while this is what sadness brought

I learnt one by one through those
Subtle smiles beneath chaos

Since then I have started offering
Full course meal when he was visiting

13. A lane behind the Hotel

Looking out of my window
On a random sunday afternoon

A drop of sweat rolls down next to my brow
Maybe this is the gate to my fortune

Tall, grey buildings all around
A brown bridge with city lights

Makes my heart pound
Maybe the future is in my sight

It all feels very similar,yet unknown
Feels like past lives were here

Makes my heart transform to flower from stone
How I conquered most of my fears

My mother would be proud of me
Was the only echo in my ear

How I wanted her here to be with me
Was the only feeling filling me with cheer

I would say, I made it mom
Knowing she believed in me since I was born

With tears rolling down my cheek
And her being the only support, I will always seek

14. Let's clear the vacuum

We sit at our place
Uncovering truths we hate to face

Maybe now nothing to say
But once, it was come what may

So much to feel
Like the giant onion ready to peel

You say " Let's clear the air"
I worry, maybe air is the only thing left there

But I do say "yes!"
Hoping to fill the vacuum with caress

We cleared the air
But it meant not to meet anywhere

I accepted as the last option
Since then I take every step with caution

15. I need some AIR

Quiet breeze on my face
Slipping into my headspace

Blessed to have it empty
To fill it with something tempting

Like the wheezing of the wind
So chaotic yet rhythmic

There's a whiff of petrichor
Who knows what's in store

The touch of wind so heavenly
Provides the peace, truly leavenly

Oh to be nurtured by it
Might make your perspective shift

Be careful! So addictive
So free yet so restrictive

Oh to be loved by air
I would say yes without any care

16. How do you describe it?

Million thoughts in mind
Still nothing yet ready to unwind

The love and grit towards a passion
Yet not able to make it to action

It's time to wake up
Filling my own half empty cup

Forcing to leave the sleep
To answer the heart's call that runs deep

It's a will to be strong
Since the journey is too long

Getting tired is easy
Some rise rough-ambition gets greasy

I will make it to the Other Side
But for now, I will enjoy the ride

Alone or with people
I will keep writing my own Sequel

17. Diary of a 21 year old

No one told me, how difficult it gets
Making a home away from home in silhouettes

New found freedom or loneliness?
Working all the way through forgetfulness

Handling little errands to big techs
It's a little too much on my decks

Sooner or later, this place feels safe
To rest even after you commit a major gaffe

And the day comes finally
As you travel back silently

Being well aware
The feeling of being at home is rare

The place where there is love
And you are enough

18. Soul-Ties

From exchanging and eating tiffin boxes
Where we forgot to look at our watches

To meeting twice a year
Our bonds became way more than dear

Even when low and down
Their motivational speech is like reclaiming a crown

One saying of "I am here, don't worry"
Making all fears and insecurities blurry

Teaching you all Good and Bad deeds
Helping us navigate through adulting needs

Where the distance and silence
Doesn't really mean non-compliance

Some bonds so old, yet so fresh
Everytime you meet them in flesh

If you also remember someone so close
Make sure to call them like a medicine dose

19. Melancholised Surprise

A message received when least expected
The moment softly reconnected

Making it all rosy
Suddenly it was all cozy

It was such a quiet ripple
That sounded like the bell of a temple

Asking, "How was your day?"
As my heart only wanted them to stay

Just said "Good:)"
When wanted to tell all that I could

Some things are better from a distance
But it was a heartthrob that instance

20. The Invisible Cage

World so wide and fierce
Hiding with all my fears

The cage of self attested expectations
Killing myself with limitations

These inhibitions, I held close
Since how long who knows

Soul is ready to pierce
But it may take years

Dancing on a road sounds fun
Till I am actually done

So difficult to not care
But I really wish to be rare

Hopefully these limits are paper-thin
And I have a match within

21. Nature's Beautiful Sieve

For long periods in my life
Felt like a huge rock in river Nile

Tried to act all tough
Piercing through water like I am rough

Forgot to see underneath
The damage leading closer to my death

River of Emotions
Hitting on me, causing all this commotion

Saw a mesh of algae next to me
Oh, water passing through so elegantly

Realising the more I resist
These problems will persist

Rather collect the learnings
Without resisting the flow of feelings